THE KING'S SINGERS' MADRIGALS

Volume 2:

European Madrigals in 5 parts

FABER MUSIC

DISTRIBUTED BY

HAL•LEONARD®

7777 W. BLUEMOUND RD. P.O. BOX 13819 MILWAUKEE, WI 53213

First published in 1984 by Faber Music Ltd
in association with Faber & Faber Ltd
3 Queen Square London WC1N 3AU
Music drawn by James Holmes
Printed in USA
All rights reserved

Music editor: Clifford Bartlett
German texts translated by Olive Sayce
Spanish text edited and translated by Jack Sage
Italian and French texts edited and translated by Sylvia Dimiziani,
Associate Professor of Music, State University of New York at Buffalo.

Grateful acknowledgment is given to the following for their advice:
Peter Butler, Peter Bartlett, Anthony Rooley and Professor Manlio Cortelazzo
of Centro di Studio per la Dialettologia Italiana, Padova.

A selection of these madrigals is recorded by the King's Singers on HMV
SLS 1078393 (2 record set), and also on tape cassette TC-SLS 1078395

CONTENTS

INTRODUCTION

The madrigal is perhaps the most satisfying form of music ever devised for recreational singing. This collection of 5-part pieces — together with the companion volume of 4-part pieces — has been drawn from the repertoire presented in the BBC Television series 'The King's Singers' Madrigal History Tour'. The choice was made to illustrate the enormous range of styles covered by the title Madrigal. It was not possible to include examples by all the best known composers, but we know that every piece in this volume is enjoyable to sing and can work well in performance.

The collections illustrate the development of the secular part-song from the Italian Frottola and Spanish Villancico of the late 15th century to the sophisticated contrapuntal style of the English madrigalists of the early 17th century. To music publishers of the period nearly all settings of secular verse came under the general heading of Madrigal, including sonnets, popular and dialect poems and ballets.

The Frottola was usually for solo voice with a simple, chordal accompaniment either for instruments or other voices. The words tended to be frivolous and often ribald. Gradually the more contrapuntal style of the Netherland composers — the *oltremontani*, men from the other side of the Alps — began to inspire a new generation of madrigal composers to seek to marry this style to the swift and supple rhythms of Italian poetry. Italy's greatest lyric poet, Petrarch, enjoyed a great revival during the 16th century and his expressive and flexible verse forms were used as models by poets and composers alike.

The first publications of madrigals in the 1530s and 1540s were highly successful, and revealed an avid market of literate and sophisticated people who relished the fashionable pastime of singing settings of poems about life and love. Each vocal line was now equally important, so that no-one with the necessary ability needed to feel left out at after-dinner entertainments.

Composers from Spain, Germany and France travelled to Italy to learn, or obtained published music to study. They adopted the madrigalists' musical style and applied it to their own vernacular poetry. In Spain the Villancico thrived well into the 16th century and was gradually developed polyphonically by Juan Vasquez and others. In Germany many composers followed the Italian style, setting Italian texts as well as German (and sometimes a mixture of the two); they also delighted in folk-song settings and satirical parodies. The French composers specialised in 'courtly love' songs and in lighter settings of the more frivolous aspects of love. In England the madrigal enjoyed a remarkable Indian Summer during the last years of the reign of Queen Elizabeth I, mainly due to the influence of one man, Thomas Morley. In his much-quoted book, *A Plaine and Easie Introduction to Practicall Musicke*, he outlined the qualities appropriate to both composers and performers of madrigals: They should be of 'an amorous humour ... sometimes wanton, sometimes drooping, sometimes grave and staid ... and the more variety [they] show the better [they] shall please!'

Many madrigals exist in more than one version, and in some cases the versions printed here are not precisely the same as those recorded by the King's Singers. They are notated with the convenience of today's singers in mind (see Editorial notes, p. 91). For example, the time signature ₵ is used consistently to indicate a two-in-a-bar feel. Similarly, archaic spellings in the texts have generally been modernised. We would recommend a close reading of each text as a first priority: many of them are riddled with lascivious double-entendres which can be exploited effectively in performance. On the other hand, we have resisted the temptation to add tempo or dynamic indications, but we hope the brief Notes to each piece will assist singers in making their own decisions on the manner of performance. It is well worth experimenting with strongly contrasted vocal colours and dynamics. We suggest that vibrato is kept to a minimum.

William Byrd wrote: 'there is not any music of instruments whatsoever, comparable to that which is made of the voices of men, where voices are good, and the same well sorted and ordered'. While, as a male voice ensemble, we would agree with him, we freely admit that mixed voice ensembles are no less appropriate! In this collection, therefore, all the pieces are set at pitches suitable for mixed choirs and vocal groups.

Simon Carrington

The King's Singers
September 1983

PERFORMANCE NOTES
AND TRANSLATIONS

1. My gracious lady, I find in the movement of your eyes a *je ne sais quoi*, an I cannot tell, which transfers all my troubles to my sad fantasy. I seek solitude for contemplation, and find in it so many pleasures that I would die, were I to go on thinking about it. But these thoughts are so frail that they soon come to an end, and I must turn to other things. Yet I persist in these same thoughts and find myself saying: if only this were not to come to an end! But then I perceive that so much pleasure is not one of those things that can last.

The long, languorous lines and rich sonorities of this sensual music convey an atmosphere of restrained passion. The tempo should not be too slow, nor the performance over-indulgent, although this style of writing can contain a wide dynamic range and a slight flexibility of tempo.

2. (1) Then let us all drink this wine with jubilation. This wine is the prince of all wines, above all other. Drink, my dear Dieterlein, then you will never be thirsty. Drink up! (2) There is still a drop at the bottom. You are a lazy drinker — tip up the glass, then it will run more freely. Drink, my dear Dieterlein, enjoy the cool wine. Drink up !

The cantus firmus in the 4th voice (baritone), where the text most easily fits the music, needs to be suitably robust and to predominate, being sung perhaps by more voices. The other parts should accompany lightly until the chorus, 'Trinks gar aus'. Make the words particularly clear and all the quaver movement exact. We have found it effective to start the second verse quietly, building a vigorous crescendo to the end. Care should be taken that all the words beginning with a vowel have a clear attack; e.g. 'gar aus'.

3. Alas, for sorrow! Must we part? Alas, woe is me, who would not feel pity? Alas for the pain I feel in my heart! If I must give you up, it will cost me my life.

Here the opening chordal section is enhanced by a certain amount of rubato to emphasise the word-stresses. The magnificent second section needs careful balancing to preserve its rich sonorities. The lower parts must be strong enough to support the gradually ascending upper two voices. The section beginning 'so kost's mir' should build relentlessly from a soft beginning with long legato lines and a lean on the discordant rather than the concordant notes. The bass entries on 'Muss' should be firm and clear with a slight accent but no vibrato!

4. (1) Dancing and springing, singing and ringing, fa la la, let lutes and fiddles join in. My whole heart is set on music-making and rejoicing. (2) Beautiful maidens in the green meadow, fa la la, to sing and pass the time with them with playful jest gladdens my heart more than silver and gold.

This witty, lively piece benefits from light, bright textures and a twinkle in the eye. Tease the cross rhythms by suggesting a 'hemiola' in both sets of "Fa la la's", and experiment with echo effects in the second set.

5. Now let the heavens rejoice, and may Mantua be proud that you have her sceptre and mantle; you who with great wisdom go forth conquering evil with good. Thus let Astrea guide your mind, and may love keep your heart open; may your golden crown be always adorned with wreaths of olive and laurel.

Or si rallegri was written in honour of the coronation of the Duke of Mantua in 1587. From the opening fanfare, the performance should reflect in bright, ringing Italian the jubilant mood of the text and the occasion, with clearly defined contrapuntal lines.

6. O valley, filled with the sound of my laments: river so often swollen by my weeping; wild beasts, wandering birds and fish restrained by verdant river banks; air made warm and limpid by my sighs; paths once sweet but now so bitter; O hills that brought me joy but now offer only pity (and yet from habit Love stills leads me here) — in all of you I see your usual beauty, but not, alas, in me. For, once a happy being, I have now become the dwelling place of infinite sorrow. From up there I used to gaze on my beloved, and by these paths I return to see the place from where her soul departed, leaving on earth her beautiful mortal remains.

This is a remarkable setting of a remarkable poem — a lament by Petrarch on the death of his beloved Laura. Performers should emphasise the contrast displayed in both words and music between the restrained sonorities conveying the poet's happy memories of the past and the impassioned cries of his present grief. Don't hesitate to exploit the word-painting and to characterise the imagery, building up the final bars to a dramatic climax.

7. (1) Let all strong soldiers come well armed. I am invincible Love, the just archer. Banish all fear, and follow me boldly, all together in perfect formation. (2) Those who oppose you seem formidable foes, but they are defenceless against one whose aim is sure. Banish all fear, and armed with strength and courage, be cunning in the battle.

Gastoldi was the originator of the *balletto*, the madrigal-form later developed so expertly by Morley — cf. No. 12. *Amor vittorioso* is a martial song in praise of love, portraying Cupid the archer as a victor in battle rather than the more traditional curly-headed cherub. This kind of homophonic piece can sound dull and uninspiring unless performed with great zest, forceful rhythmic drive, very precise ensemble and sharply contrasting dynamics.

8. The bass text means: 'Never trust a hunchback; the same goes for a cripple. If a braggart be good, write about it in the history books.' The other parts imitate animal noises in 'beastly counterpoint': Woof-woof, meow, hoo, cuckoo. Fa la la.

This well-known show-stopper lends itself to a number of extra-musical effects! As a guide, we make the following suggestions: sing the 'Fa la la's in a mock-serious style; give the bass Cantus Firmus with its phoney moral a pompous manner and convey increasing annoyance at the beastly interruptions; meanwhile, let the animals compete for attention and become ever more frantically insistent, ending in a cacophony of farmyard sounds. The final 'Fa la la' could imply a reconciliation. The animal sounds can be freely interpreted, though they should be pitched accurately!

9. Zephyr returns, bringing back the fair weather, grass and flowers, and all his gentle company, the chirping of Procne and Philomel's lament, and springtime's white and scarlet array. Meadows sparkle as the sky brightens, and Jove delights to see his daughter again; love fills the air, water and all the earth, as every creature renews love's desire. But for me, alas, only sorrowful sighs return, wrenched from the depths of my heart by the one who took its keys away to Heaven. For me the song of birds and the flowering hillsides are empty as a barren desert, and innocent, lovely maidens in their gentle movements seem harsh, savage creatures.

This is a setting of another of Petrarch's laments on the death of Laura. The poem must have had a personal relevance for Monteverdi whose own wife died at around the time he set these words, adding to the misery of his years in Mantua. There should be a strong contrast between the gentle images of spring in the triple time sections and the dark, intense colours of the quadruple. The final passage builds from a quiet start, pushing forward to the final agonising climax. The time changes can be treated flexibly and the slow sections must not be allowed to drag. Care needs to be taken that the semi-quaver passages sound more like the gentle spring Zephyr of the title than a raging hurricane. Other modern editions have omitted the continuo part; it is not essential, but if a harpsichord (or even better, a lute) is available, it will clarify the harmony as well as contribute another tone character.

10. Our sad parting caused me such grief. My body was colder than marble; numbed by sorrow and unfeeling as a tree, my face was drained of all its colour.

This melancholy expression of the sadness of parting is almost self-indulgent in its unrelieved desolation. The contrapuntal entries should be clearly defined, and the rising scales in the final section should be heard passing through the voices as the vocal colours become ever more dry and pallid to match the imagery of the poem. The original edition is somewhat unsatisfactory in its notation of accidentals and word-underlay, so feel free to change our suggestions.

11. (1) Good morning. So now, what news have we? Shouldn't I expect some from you? If you don't tell me quickly, I'll make a bit of news myself. Well, since you are so stubborn, good eventide, good night, good evening, good day. (2) If you gather some currants, bring some to me. For I am eager to see everything, but especially to see you some morning, dear maidens. Good day.

Judge the speed of this sparkling song of greeting from the frenetic middle section, letting the words 'Bon jour' ring out clearly. There are opportunities for vocal colour in the progression from 'Bon jour' to 'Bon soir', where the piece can effectively be put to sleep with a *ritenuto* — followed immediately by an *a tempo*.

12. This popular and much performed madrigal is curiously difficult to perform well, and is by no means as easy as it looks. It demands a fast and lively tempo, absolute clarity, a very careful balance and singing that is light and precise, particularly in the two rather angular tenor parts. Dare we suggest that familiarity should not be allowed to breed contempt for this miniature masterpiece? Don't ignore a slight, suggestive undertone in the 'Fa la la's!

13. Establish a rich, blended texture while being careful to maintain a direct, clear sound, especially in the lower voices. Allow the sense to run over the rests where the text demands, and use the smooth line of the running crotchet movement to keep the haunting last phrase moving.

14. This is very often sung as a simple, pretty piece — an interpretation which belies the bitterness expressed in the poem and the biting sting in the tail. Keep the tempo flowing and allow the top line to bear the responsibility for the lyric.

15. The 'Fa la la' refrains in this madrigal are in direct contrast to those in, for instance, *Now is the month of Maying*, and express an unusual mood of heavy melancholy, requiring a weighty stress to preserve the feeling of despair. The words 'Now chanting go and singing' are surely laced with a bitter sarcasm.

1. Gentil señora mía

JUAN BOSCAN ALMOGAVER

JUAN VASQUEZ
(c. 1510 - 1560)

si es-to no a-ca-ba - - - - - se. Mas, des-pués ve - -

- to no a - - ca - - - - ba - - se. Mas,

es - - to no a-ca - - - ba - - - - - se. Mas, des - - - - pués ve - -

a - ca - - ba - - - - - se._____ Mas, des - -

a - ca - ba - - se. Mas, des - - - - pués ve - -

- o que tan - - to go - zar No

des-pués ve - - - - - o que tan - to_____ go - - zar No es

- o que tan - to _____ go - zar, que tan - - to _____ go - zar, No es

- - pués ve - - - - o que tan - - to go - zar, No es de las

- o que tan - - to go - zar, No es de

2. So trinken wir alle

ARNOLD VON BRUCK
(c. 1500 - 1554)

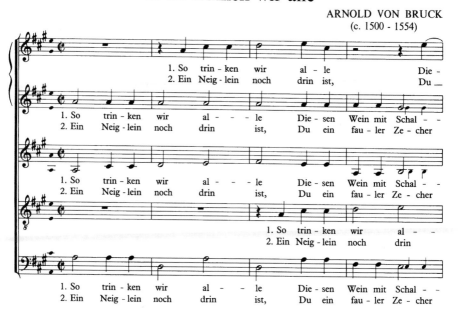

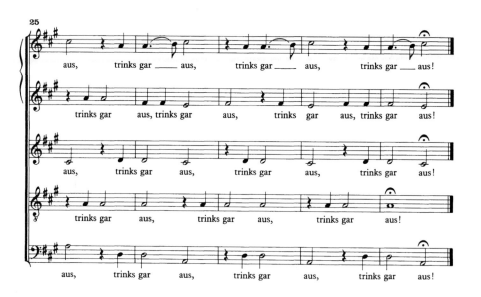

3. Ach, weh des Leiden

HANS LEO HASSLER
(1564 - 1612)

Ach, weh des Lei - den, Muß es dann sein ge - schei - den?

Ach, weh mir Ar - men, Wen sollt's doch nicht er - bar - men?

4. Tanzen und Springen
(Gagliarda)

HANS LEO HASSLER
(1564 - 1612)

5. Or si rallegri il cielo

MUTIO MANFREDI

GIACHES DE WERT
(1535 - 1596)

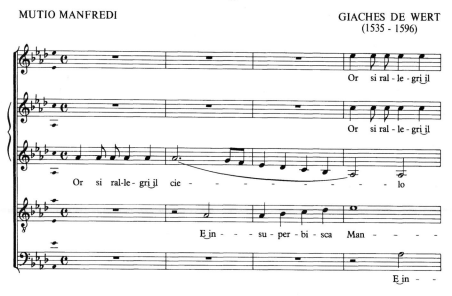

Or si ral - le - gri il
Or si ral - le - gri il
Or si ral-le - gri il cie - - - - - - - lo
E in - - - su - per - bi - sca Man - - - -
E in - -

cie - - - - - - - lo E in-su - per - bi - sca Man - -
cie - - - - - - - lo E in-su - per - bi - sca Man - -
e in - su - - per - bi - sca Man - -
- to, Or si ral -
- su - per - bi - sca Man - - - to,

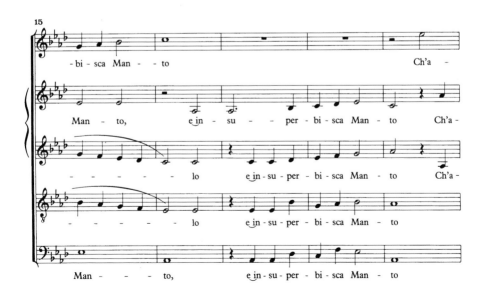

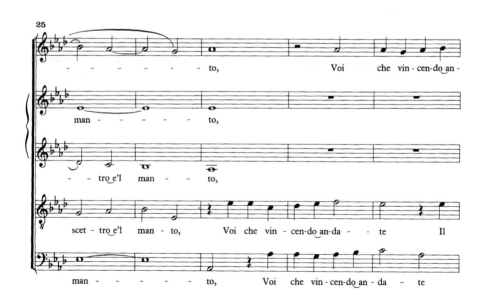

6. Valle, che de' lamenti miei se' piena

FRANCESCO PETRARCA
(1304 - 1374)

GIACHES DE WERT
(1535 - 1596)

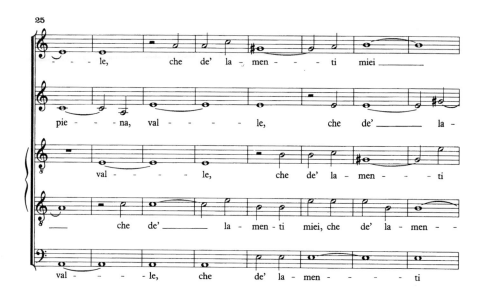

108

116

144

me — na, ov' an - cor per u - san-za A - mor mi me — na;

_ mi me — — na; _

- mor mi me — na; _

per u - san — za, ov' an - cor per u - san-za A - mor mi me — na;

- mor mi me — na, A - mor mi me — — — — na;

149 *Seconda Parte*

Ben ri - co - no - sco in voi l'u - sa - te for — — — me, Non, _

Ben ri - co - no - sco in voi l'u - sa - te for — — — me, Non,

Non,

Ben ri - co - no - sco in voi l'u - sa - te for — me, Non,

Non,

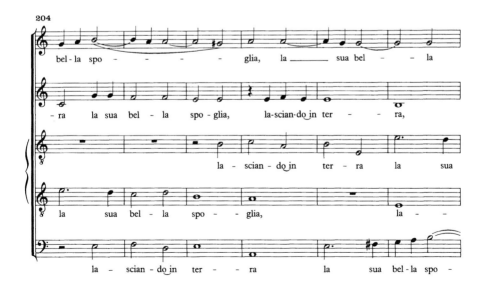

7. Amor vittorioso
(Tutti venite armati)

GIOVANNI GIACOMO GASTOLDI
(c. 1550 - 1622)

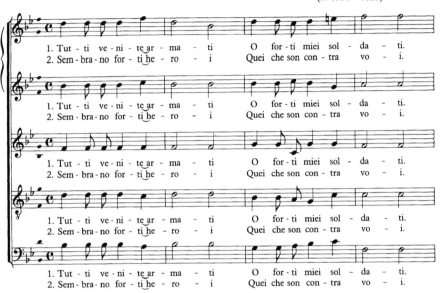

1. Tut - ti ve - ni - te ar - ma - ti   O for - ti miei sol - da - ti.
2. Sem - bra - no for - ti he - ro - i   Quei che son con - tra vo - i.

Fa la la la la la la, fa la la la la la.

1. Io son l'in-vit - t' A - mo - re Giu - sto sa - et - ta - to - re. Non te - me - te
2. Ma da chi sa fe - ri - re, Non si sa - pran scher-mi - re. Non te - me - te

1. Io son l'in-vit - t' A - mo - re Giu - sto sa - et - ta - to - re. Non te - me - te
2. Ma da chi sa fe - ri - re, Non si sa - pran scher-mi - re. Non te - me - te

1. Io son l'in-vit - t' A - mo - re Non te - me - te
2. Ma da chi sa fe - ri - re, Non te - me - te

1. Giu - sto sa - et - ta - to - re. Non te - me - te
2. Non si sa - pran scher-mi - re. Non te - me - te

1. Io son l'in-vit - t' A - mo - re Giu - sto sa - et - ta - to - re. Non te - me - te
2. Ma da chi sa fe - ri - re, Non si sa - pran scher-mi - re. Non te - me - te

pun - to, Ma in bel-la schie-ra u - ni - ti, Me se-gui-ta-te ar - di - ti.
pun - to, Ma co-ra-ggio-si e for - ti, Siat' a la pu-gna ac-cor - ti.

pun - to, Ma in bel-la schie-ra u - ni - ti, Me se-gui-ta-te ar - di - ti.
pun - to, Ma co-ra-ggio-si e for - ti, Siat' a la pu-gna ac-cor - ti.

pun - to, Ma in bel-la schie-ra u - ni - ti, Me se-gui-ta-te ar - di - ti.
pun - to, Ma co-ra-ggio-si e for - ti, Siat' a la pu-gna ac-cor - ti.

pun - to, Ma in bel-la schie-ra u - ni - ti, Me se-gui-ta-te ar - di - ti.
pun - to, Ma co-ra-ggio-si e for - ti, Siat' a la pu-gna ac-cor - ti.

pun - to, Ma in bel-la schie-ra u - ni - ti, Me se-gui-ta-te ar - di - ti.
pun - to, Ma co-ra-ggio-si e for - ti, Siat' a la pu-gna ac-cor - ti.

8. Contrapunto bestiale alla mente

ADRIANO BANCHIERI
(1568 - 1634)

29

Fa la la la la la la la la la la la la la, fa la la la la la

Fa la la la la la la la la la la la la la, fa la la la la la

Fa la la la la la la la la la la la la la, fa la la la la la

Fa la la la la la la la la la, fa la la la la la

Fa la la la la la la la la la, fa la la la la la

35

la la la la, fa la la la la la la la la la.

la la la la la la la la, fa la la la la la la la la la.

la la la la la la la la, fa la la la la la la la la.

la la la la, fa la la la la la la la la la.

la la la la, fa la la la la la la la la la.

9. Zefiro torna e'l bel tempo rimena

FRANCESCO PETRARCA
(1304 - 1374)

CLAUDIO MONTEVERDI
(1567 - 1643)

25

32

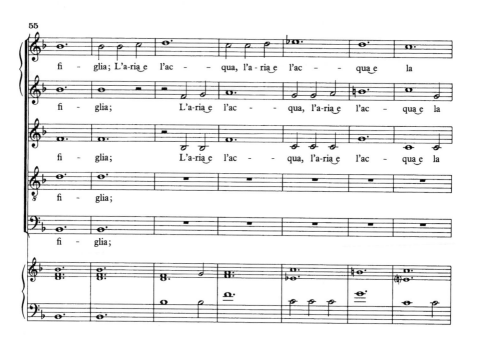

au - gel - let - ti e fio-rir, e fio-rir piag - - ge, E'n bel - le

E can - tar au - gel - let - ti e fio-rir piag - - ge, E'n bel - le don - n'o - ne -

- let - - - ti e fio - rir_____ piag - - ge, E'n bel - le don - n'o -

- tar au - gel - let - - - ti e fio-rir piag - - ge, E'n bel - le don - n'o -

101

don - n'o - ne - ste at - ti so - a - - vi So - - no,

- ste at - - ti so - a - - vi So - - no,

- ne - - ste at - ti so - a - - vi So - no, so - no un de -

- ne - - ste at - ti so - a - - vi So - - no, so - -

10. Triste départ

NICOLAS GOMBERT
(c. 1500 - 1556)

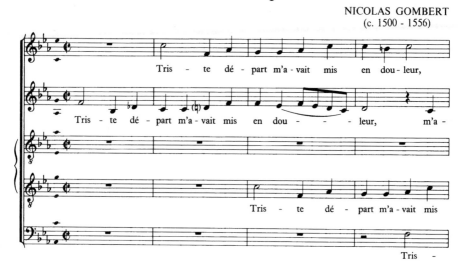

11. Bon jour; et puis, quelles nouvelles?

CLEMENT MAROT
(? 1496 - 1544)

ORLANDE DE LASSUS
(1532 - 1594)

23

nuit, bon soir, bon soir, bon jour, _____ bon

nuit, bon soir, bon soir, _____ bon jour, _

bon - ne nuit, bon soir, bon soir, _____ bon jour,

bon - ne nuit, bon soir, bon soir, _____ bon jour, bon _____

bon - ne nuit, bon soir, bon soir, _____ bon

28

jour, bon jour, bon jour, bon jour, bon jour, bon jour.

bon _____ jour, bon _____ jour, _____ bon jour.

bon jour, bon jour, bon _____ jour, bon jour.

jour, bon jour, bon jour, bon jour. _____

jour, bon jour, bon jour, bon jour.

33

37

car pour tout ___ voir, je suis gros, je suis gros, je suis gros: Mais c'est

___ pour tout voir, je suis gros, je suis gros, je suis gros, je suis gros: Mais c'est

tout voir, car pour tout voir, je suis gros, je suis gros, je suis gros, je suis gros:

voir, car pour tout voir, je suis gros, je suis gros, je suis gros: Mais c'est de ___

voir, car pour tout voir, je suis gros, je suis gros: Mais c'est de

de vous voir, mais ___ c'est de vous voir quelque matin, Mes da-moi-sel-

de vous voir, mais c'est de vous voir quel-que ma-tin, quel-que ma-tin, Mes damoisel-

Mais c'est, mais c'est de vous voir quel-que matin, quelque ma-tin, Mes damoisel-

___ vous voir, mais c'est de vous voir quel-que matin, Mes damoi-sel - - les,

vous voir, mais c'est de vous voir quel-que ma-tin, Mes damoisel-

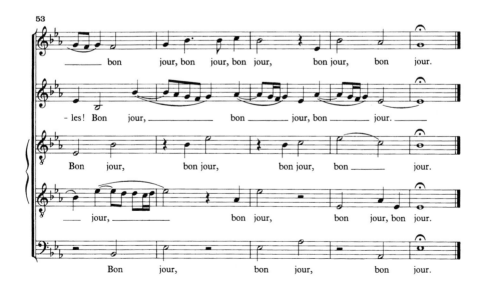

12. Now is the month of Maying

THOMAS MORLEY
(1557/8 - 1602)

(8)

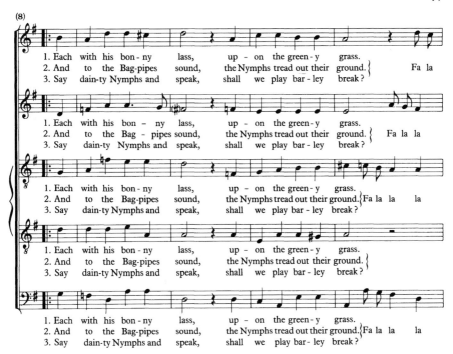

1. Each with his bon - ny lass, up - on the green-y grass.
2. And to the Bag-pipes sound, the Nymphs tread out their ground. } Fa la
3. Say dain-ty Nymphs and speak, shall we play bar - ley break?

1. Each with his bon - ny lass, up - on the green-y grass.
2. And to the Bag - pipes sound, the Nymphs tread out their ground. } Fa la la
3. Say dain-ty Nymphs and speak, shall we play bar - ley break?

1. Each with his bon - ny lass, up - on the green - y grass.
2. And to the Bag-pipes sound, the Nymphs tread out their ground. }Fa la la la
3. Say dain-ty Nymphs and speak, shall we play bar - ley break?

1. Each with his bon - ny lass, up - on the green - y grass.
2. And to the Bag-pipes sound, the Nymphs tread out their ground. }
3. Say dain-ty Nymphs and speak, shall we play bar - ley break?

1. Each with his bon - ny lass, up - on the green - y grass.
2. And to the Bag-pipes sound, the Nymphs tread out their ground. }Fa la la la
3. Say dain-ty Nymphs and speak, shall we play bar - ley break?

13

la la la, fa la la la la la la la, fa la la la.

la la, fa la la la la, fa la la la la la la.

la, fa la la la, fa la la la la, fa la la la.

Fa la la la la, ___ fa la la la la la, la la.

la, fa la la la la la, fa la la la la la.

13. O grief ev'n on the bud

THOMAS MORLEY
(1557/8 - 1602)

1. O grief ev'n on the bud that fair-ly flower-ed The sun hath lower-ed.
2. And ah that breast which Love durst ne-ver ven-ture Bold death did en-ter.

- ed The sun hath lower - - ed. - ter. Pi -
- ture Bold death did en - -

14. The silver swan

ORLANDO GIBBONS
(1583 - 1625)

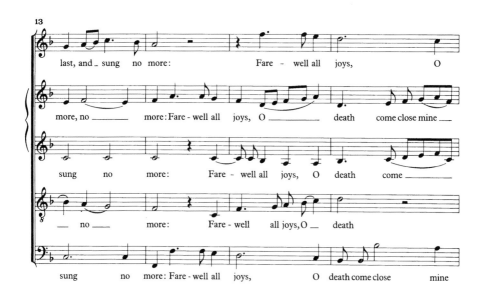

death come close mine eyes; More geese than swans now live, more fools than wise.

eyes; More geese than swans now live, more fools than wise, than ___ wise.

close mine eyes; More geese than swans ___ now live, more fools than wise.

come close mine eyes; More geese than swans now live, more fools ___ than ___ wise.

eyes; More geese than swans now live, more fools than wise.

15. Too much I once lamented

To my ancient, and much reverenced master, William Byrd

THOMAS TOMKINS
(1572 - 1656)

Too ___ much ___

Too ___ much ___ I once la - men - - - - - - ted,

Too much I once la - men - - - - - - ted, la -

Too much I once la - - men - - - - - - -

Too

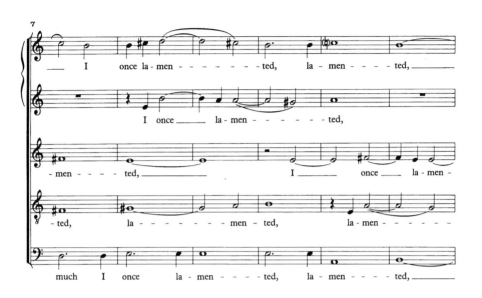

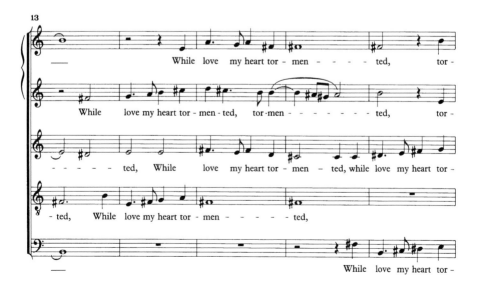

-men - - - - ted, tor - men - - - - ted, tor - men - - ted.

-men - - - - ted, tor - men - - - - ted, tor - men - - - - ted.

-men - - - ted, tor - men - - - - ted, tor - men - - - - - - - ted.

tor - men - - - - - - - ted, tor - - men - - - ted.

-men - - - - ted, tor - - - - men - - - - ted. _____

Fa la la la la la la la,

Fa la la la la la la la, fa la la la la,

Fa la la la la la la, fa la la la la la la,

Fa la la la la la la la,

Fa la la la la la la la la la la la la, fa la la la la la la la la la la la,

Soprano I and Soprano II exchange parts for repeat.

* Small notes for second time only.

Soprano I and Soprano II exchange parts for repeat.

EDITORIAL NOTES

This performing edition aims to present the music in notation that will be readily understood by singers today. Word texts have been carefully edited and presented in modern orthography. Since all these madrigals are available in standard musicological editions, it has not been thought necessary to print a detailed critical commentary. Editorial accidentals are printed in small type, and all accidentals apply throughout the bar. Some apparently superfluous small-type accidentals arise through transposition. For example, no. 1 was originally in G minor with a key signature of one flat. Rather than use a key signature of one sharp when transposing to A minor, we have inserted individual accidentals. Thus an editorial E flat in the original is represented in the transposed version by an F with a small-print natural sign.

For each piece, the following information is set out below: source | original clefs | original key signature | original time signature | the note reduction adopted in this edition (if applicable) | the degree of transposition (if applicable) | principal variants. Minor adjustments — such as correcting obvious errors and adjusting note lengths of final chords — have been made tacitly.

Clefs are abbreviated as follows:

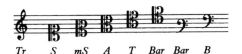

Tr   *S*   *mS*   *A*   *T*   *Bar* *Bar*   *B*

1. Vasquez: Villancicos y canciones, 1551. *SATBarB* | ♭ | C | ½
2. Schoene auszerlesne Lieder, 1536. *SSTTB* | ♭ | ¢ | ½ | up third
3. Hassler: Lustgarten, 1601. *TrSmSABar* | ♭ | C3 C | ½ bars 1-15 | E♭s bars 31-4 editorial
4. Hassler: Lustgarten, 1601. *TrSmSABar* | none | C3 | ½
5. Wert: Il nono libro, 1589. *SAATB* | ♭ | C | up minor third | bar 22: Wert prints "la scettr' e'l manto", our edition follows the author's separate edition of his poems, *Madrigali di Mutio Manfredi il Fermo*, Venice, 1606. Bar 27: Manfredi prints VINcendo, drawing attention to the pun on the name of the new Duke Vincenzo Gonzaga.
6. Wert: Il nono libro, 1589. *SATTB* | ♭ | ¢ | up tone
7. Gastoldi: Balletti, 1591. *TrTrmSAT* | none | C | down tone
8. Banchieri: Festino nella sera de giovedi grasso avanti cena, 1608. *SmSAT* | none | Θ_2^3 C | ½ | Banchieri changes time at b.12. 13-28: upper parts exchanged.
9. Monteverdi: Il sesto libro, 1614. *SSATB* | ♭ | C3 C 3 | Underlay of bars 5-7 has been emended. Bars 85-6 T "tragge" for "quella" Bars 99-102 SI "E'n bella donna honesti", SII "E'n belle donn' honesti".
10. Le cincquiesme livre, 1544. *TrmSAABar* | ♭ | ¢ | ½ | down tone | Editorial accidentals in bars 1-11 and 30-34 follow the hint of Lassus in his mass based on this chanson, who gives E♭ in bar 1 alto, bar 30 soprano and bar 32 bass. But these sections can be performed ignoring the editorial D flats. TI 16-17; repeat of "Le marbre" editorial.
11. Lassus: Livre de chansons nouvelles, 1571. *TrmSAABar* | ♭ | ¢ | ½ | down tone
12. Morley: The first books of balletts, 1595. *SATTB* | none | C
13. Morley: Canzonets, 1597. *SmSATB* | ♭ | C
14. Gibbons: The first set of madrigals and mottets, 1612. *SmSATB* | ♭ | C
15. Tomkins: Songs of 3, 4, 5 and 6 parts, 1622. *SSATB* | ♭ | ¢ | up tone | Bars 46-7 T "and Ay me"

PRONUNCIATION GUIDE

FRENCH

a	up; before final s = father; à = up; â = father; ai = let except at end of word = late; au = rope. See also note 3 below.
e	before consonant in same syllable or 2 consonants = let; at end of syllable = garden; final unstressed e, es, ent = garden; è, ê = let; é = late; eau = rope; ei = let; eu, eû = mouthshape for 'oh' but say 'ee'. See also note 3 below
i	feet; before vowel = year. See also note 3 below.
o	cause; before s and at end of word = rope; ô = rope; oeu = mouthshape for 'oh' but say 'ee'; oi = wah; ou = soon except before vowel = w. See also note 3 below
u	u, û = mouthshape for 'oo' but say 'ee'; before vowel = year. See also note 3 below
b	before c, s, t = p
c	k except before e, i, y = ss; ç = ss; ch = shame
d	
g	go except before e, i, y = vision; gn = onion
h	usually silent
j	vision
l	after i and at end of word = year
nt	usually silent at end of word
qu	k
s	ss except between vowels or when elided = z; silent at end of word; est = eh (silent 'st')
th	t
v	
w	
x	silent at end of word
y	feet except before vowel = year
z	

GERMAN

a	father; before 2 consonants = up; ä = late; au = owl
e	late; before 2 consonants or at end of word = let; ei = height; eu = oil
i	feet; before 2 consonants = wind; ie = feet
o	rope; before 2 consonants = pause
u	soon; before 2 consonants = put; ü = French u
b	at end of word = p
c	k; ch = loch (Scottish)
d	at end of word = t
g	go except at end of word = k
h	silent after vowel
j	year
qu	kv
s	ss except before vowel = z; sch = shame; at start of syllable sp = shp, st = sht
th	t
v	f
w	v
z	its

NOTES

1 Consonants sound as in English unless indicated otherwise. Double consonants in Italian are given extra stress.

2 Vowels in English are often sounded as diphthongs, e.g. *I may go = ai mei gou*. In other languages vowels sounds must be kept constant for their full duration.

3 In French the letter *m* or *n* after a vowel or diphthong is not sounded but makes the vowel nasal, i.e. adds a touch of *ng*. (The same applies sometimes to *nt* at the end of a word.) The following are all nasalized: *am, an, ean, em, en* = **ah**; *aim, ain, eim, ein, im, in* = **eh**; *ien, yen* = **ee-eh**; *om, on* = **oh**; *oin* = **weh**; *um, un* = mouthshape for 'aw' but say 'eh'.

4 French is often liased. When the ensuing word begins with a vowel, sound the final consonant of the previous word even if it is usually silent: *Elle est ici avec un homme* would sound *elleteesseeavecunom*.

5 In Italian and Spanish, all vowels must be pronounced, even when two are written to be sung on one note.

6 Accents on vowels in Italian and Spanish indicate stress and do not change the sound.

PRONUNCIATION GUIDE

	ITALIAN	SPANISH
a	father	father
e	late; before 2 consonants or at end of word = let	late
i	feet	feet
o	rope; sometimes = pause	rope
u	soon	soon
c	k except before e, i = church; ch = k	k except before e, i = th
g	go except before e, i = jam; gh = go; gl = million; gn = onion	go except before e, i = loch; gue = gabble; gui = giggle
h	silent	
j		before e, i = thin
ll		lyi
ñ		onion
qu	queen	k
s	ss except between vowels or before b, g, m, v = z; sc before e or i = shame	always ss (never z)
z	zz = its	thin